Let's Explore

A mathematics activity book

Betty Coombs   Lalie Harcourt

Illustrated by
Graham Bardell

 Addison-Wesley Publishers

Don Mills, Ontario • Reading, Massachusetts
Menlo Park, California • New York
Wokingham, England • Amsterdam • Bonn
Sydney • Singapore • Tokyo
Madrid • San Juan

Willow   Dill   Pepper   Juniper

I have curly hair.
I am not wearing green.
I am taller than Dill.
Who am I?

I am wearing green.
I am not standing.
I have straight hair.
Who am I?

I am not standing.
I am wearing orange.
I am wearing a pattern
necklace.
Who am I?

I do not have curly hair.
I am wearing green.
I am almost as tall
as Willow.
Who am I?

Read the clues with the child. Have the child examine the pictures of the
Burritts to find the character described. The child answers the question by
printing the character's name.

This farm is the Burritts' new home.
They were blown away from their
old home by a wind storm.
They now live in the apple tree.
Find the 4 Burritts, Mugwort
the mouse, Haggis the dog, and Trouble the cat.

Discuss the picture and descriptions with the child. Have her or him find
the hidden characters and the Burritts' home.

How many ways can each animal get to the Burritts' apple tree?

Haggis   Mugwort   Trouble

2   Have the child use a different color to mark the path(s) of each character. To extend the activity you might ask, **Will the animals ever meet? Which do you think is Mugwort's shortest path?** Or, **If each animal left at the same time which one would arrive at the apple tree first? Why?**

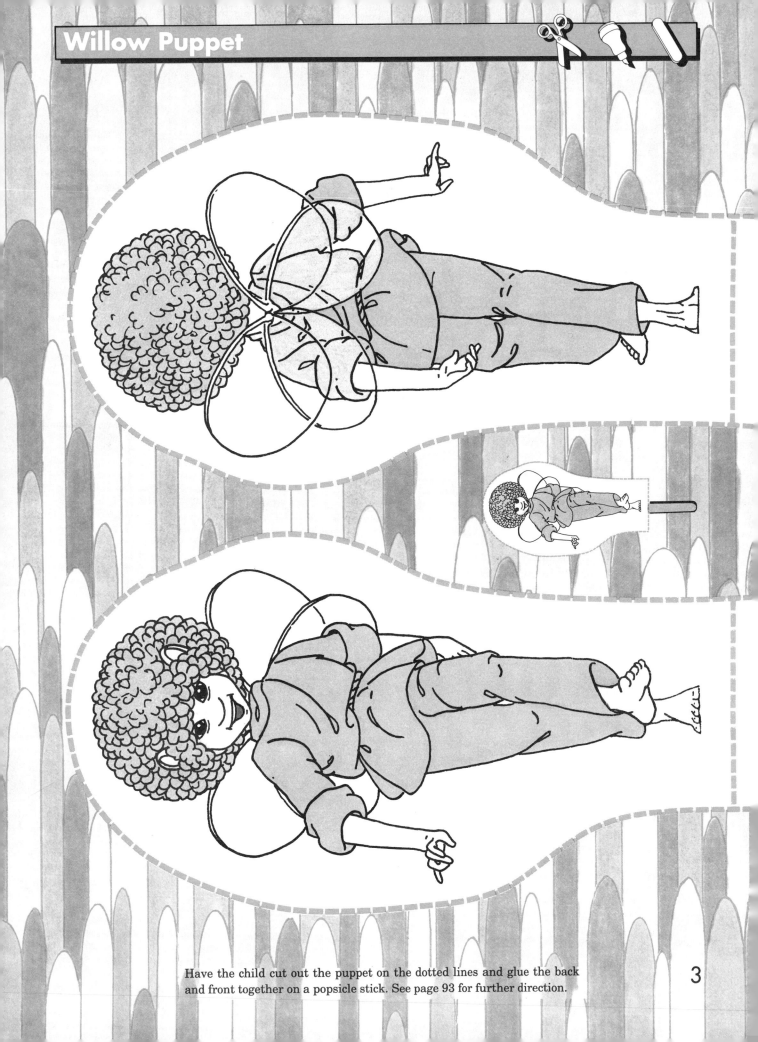

Have the child cut out the puppet on the dotted lines and glue the back and front together on a popsicle stick. See page 93 for further direction.

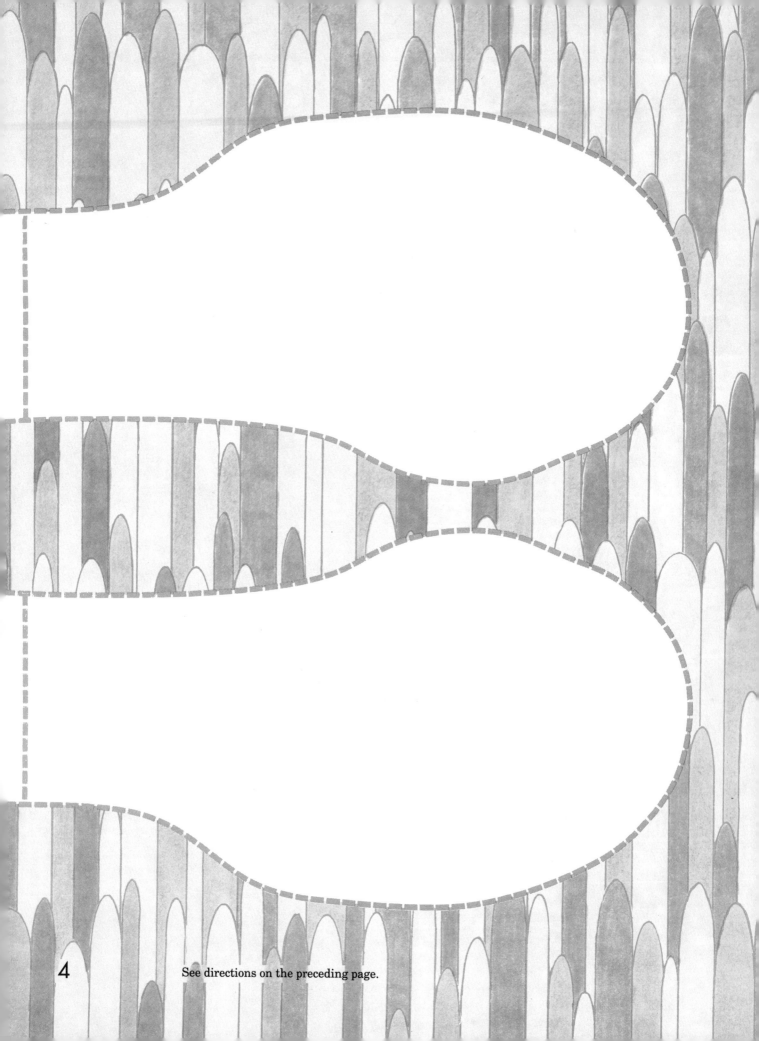

4   See directions on the preceding page.

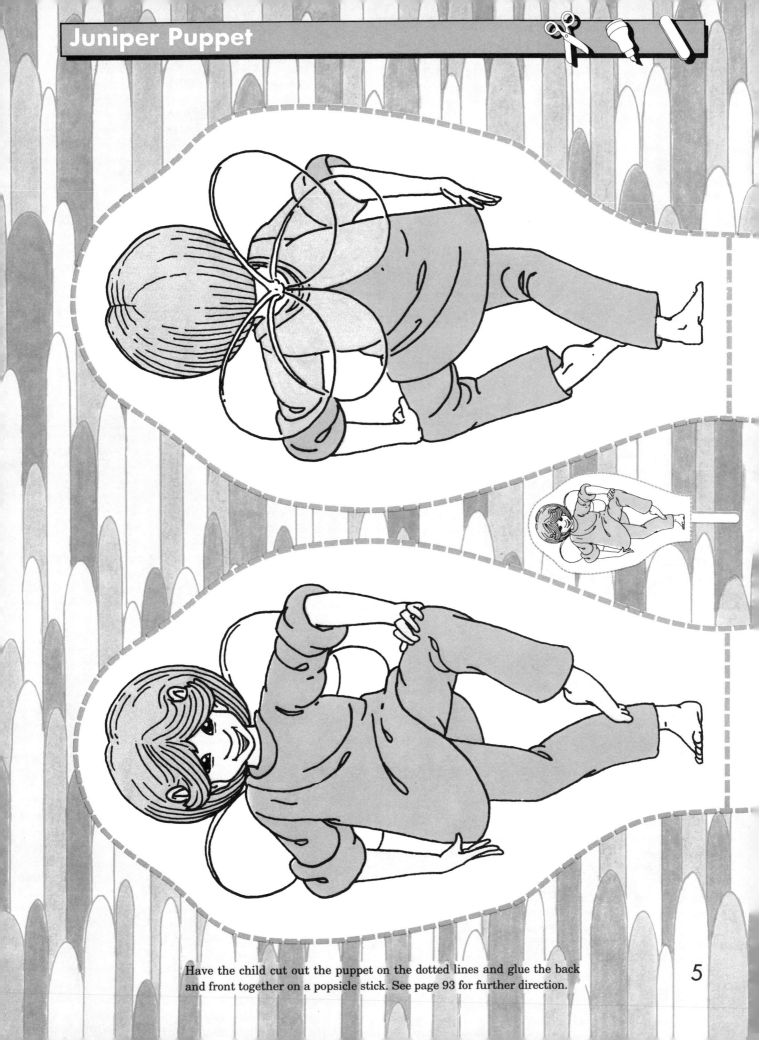

Have the child cut out the puppet on the dotted lines and glue the back and front together on a popsicle stick. See page 93 for further direction.

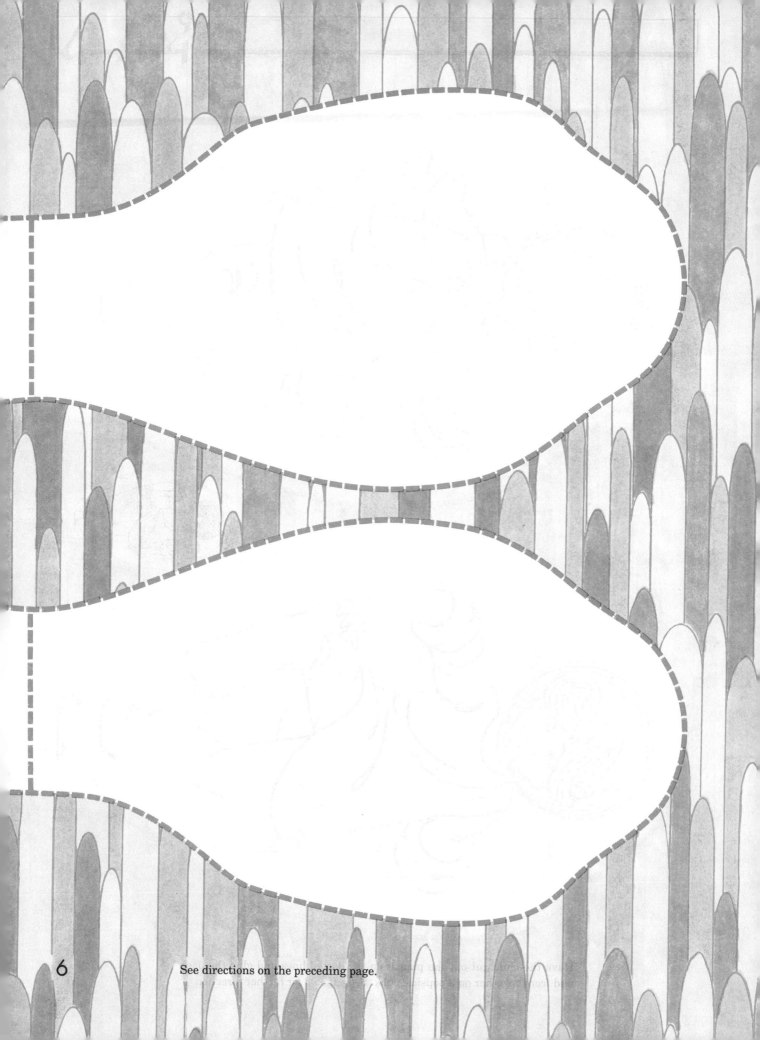

See directions on the preceding page.

Have the child cut out each puppet on the dotted lines and glue the back
and front together on a popsicle stick. See page 93 for further direction.

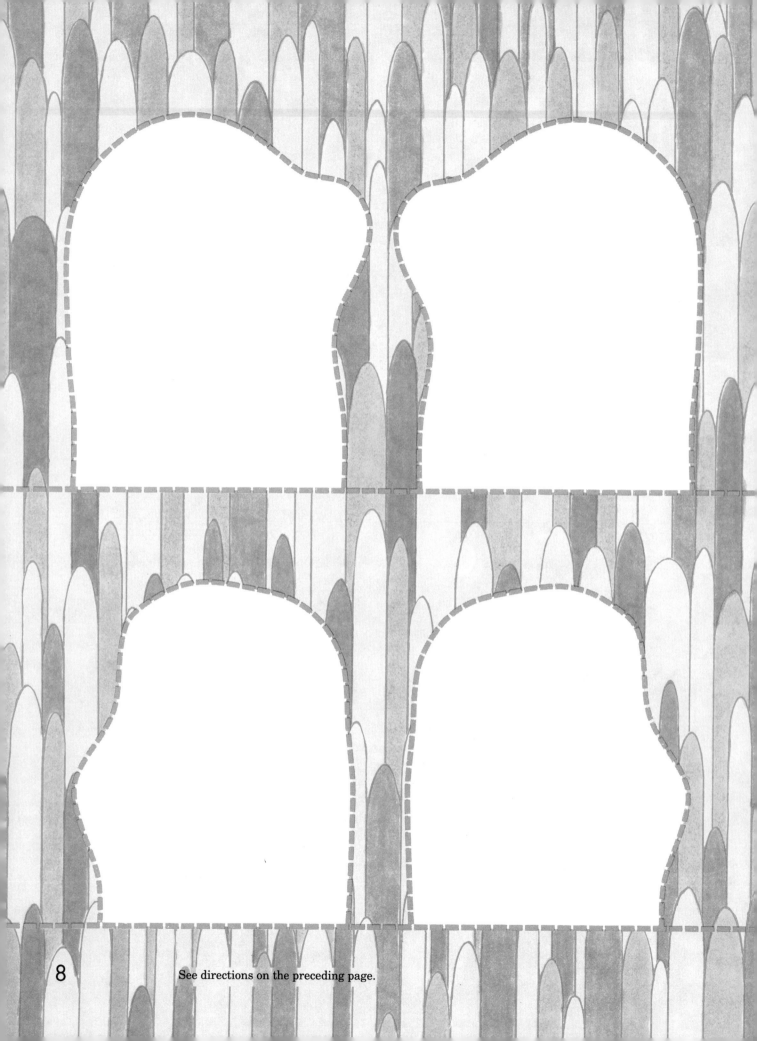

8   See directions on the preceding page.

Have the child cut out each puppet on the dotted lines and glue the back
and front together on a popsicle stick. See page 93 for further direction.

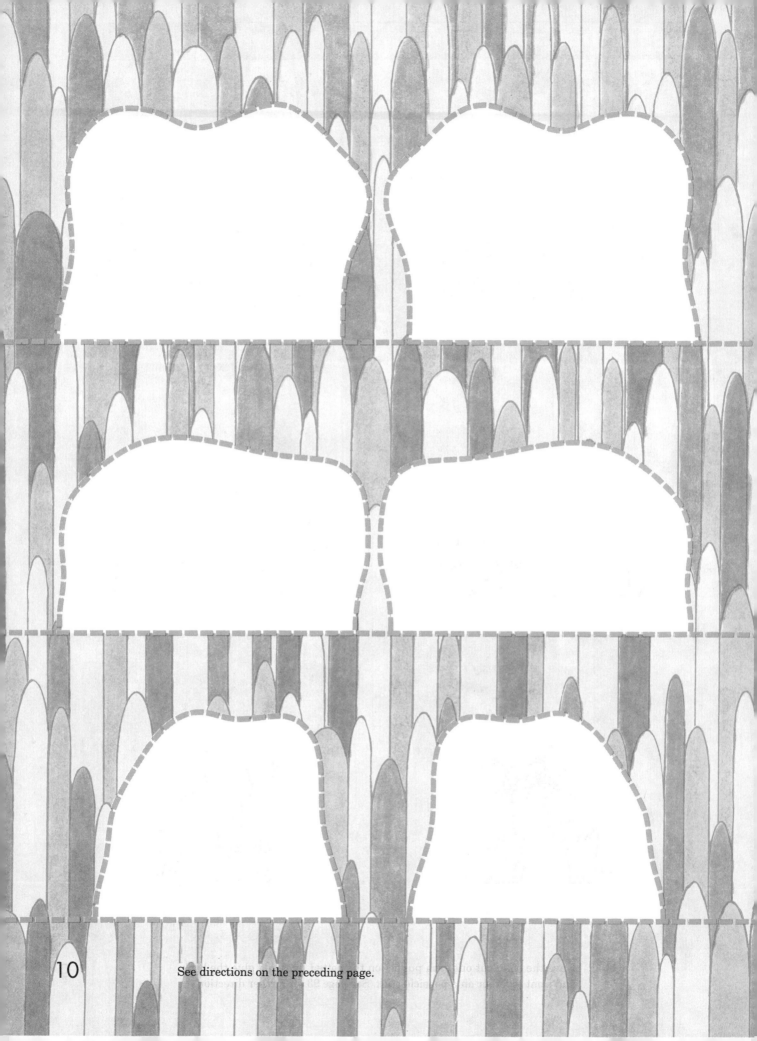

10   See directions on the preceding page.

Burritts have pets called zogs.

Have the child cut out the pictures of the zogs. You may wish to store these in an envelope. See page 93 for further direction.

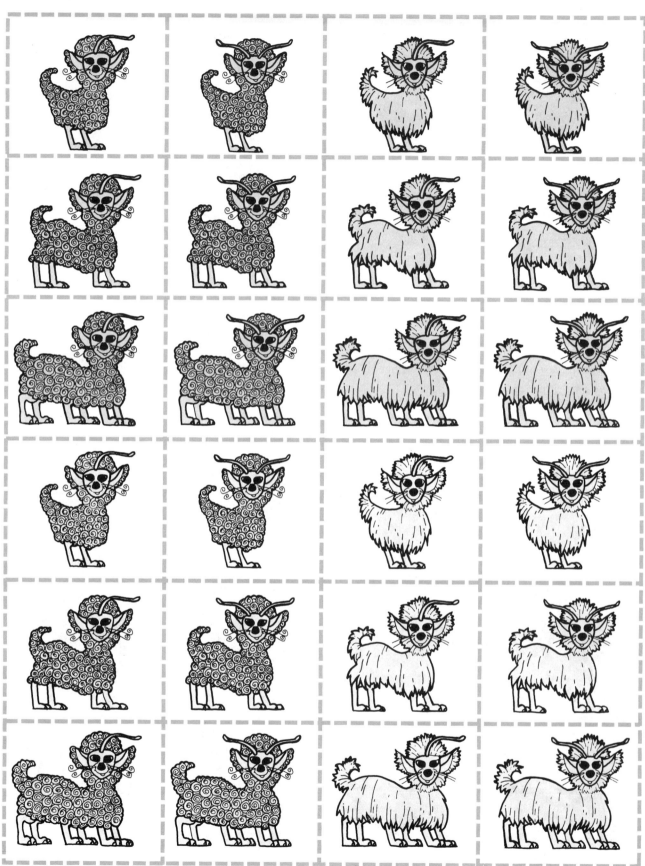

See directions on the preceding page.

These are zogs.

These are zogs.

These are not zogs.

These are not zogs.

Is this a zog? _____

Why? _____

_____

_____

_____

Is this a zog? _____

Why? _____

_____

_____

_____

Have the child examine the similarities of the sets of zogs and respond to
the questions. To extend the activity, the child might like to create her or
his own unusual pet and describe its various attributes.

Dill makes round things
for their home.
What might he make?

Willow collects colorful
shiny things.
What might she collect?

Zogs eat red juicy things.
What might they eat?

Trouble chases small
green things.
What might she chase?

There are many ways a child can respond to this page, e.g., draw, print, or cut and paste pictures from magazines or catalogs. To extend the activity, a child might like to create her or his own mystery set and ask others to guess the sorting rule.

Wallpaper Patterns

Have the child cut out the squares on the dotted lines to make wallpaper patterns on page 17. You may wish to store these in an envelope.

15

Wallpaper Patterns

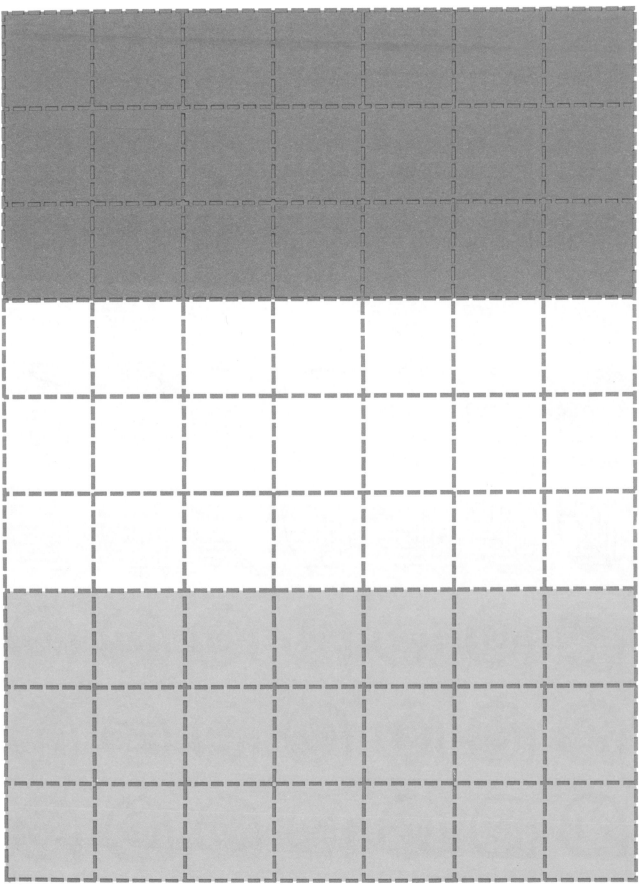

16

See directions on the preceding page.

Wallpaper Patterns

Finish this wallpaper pattern.

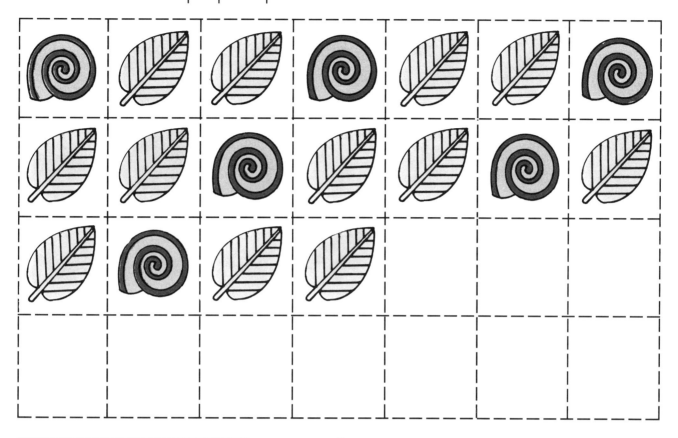

Make your own wallpaper pattern.

Have the child use the squares from pages 15 and 16 to extend the wallpaper pattern at the top of the page. Encourage the child to create and describe her or his own pattern using the remaining squares. The child might explore her or his home for other examples of patterns.

Today we found 7 nuts.
Some were acorns.
Some were walnuts.

Print the possible number sentences.

$$4 + 3 = 7$$

Yesterday we found 8 leaves.
Some were red.
Some were yellow.

Print the possible number sentences.

$$2 + 6 = 8$$

Draw a story for $7 + 0 = 7$.

Have the child use the pictures cut from pages 19 and 20 to make and record the possible number sentences.

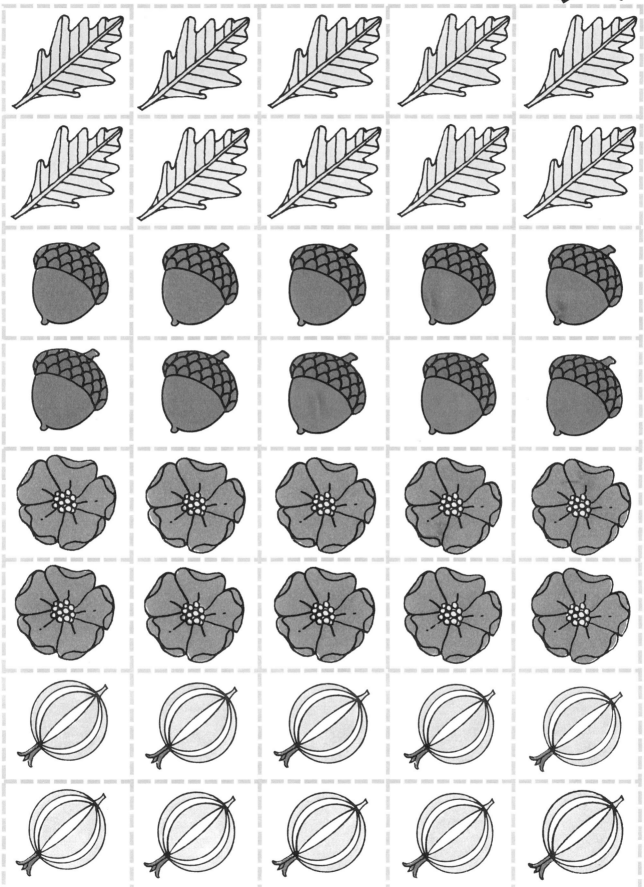

Have the child cut out the objects to generate number sentences for pages 18, 21, 22, and 23. You may wish to store these in an envelope. See page 93 for further direction.

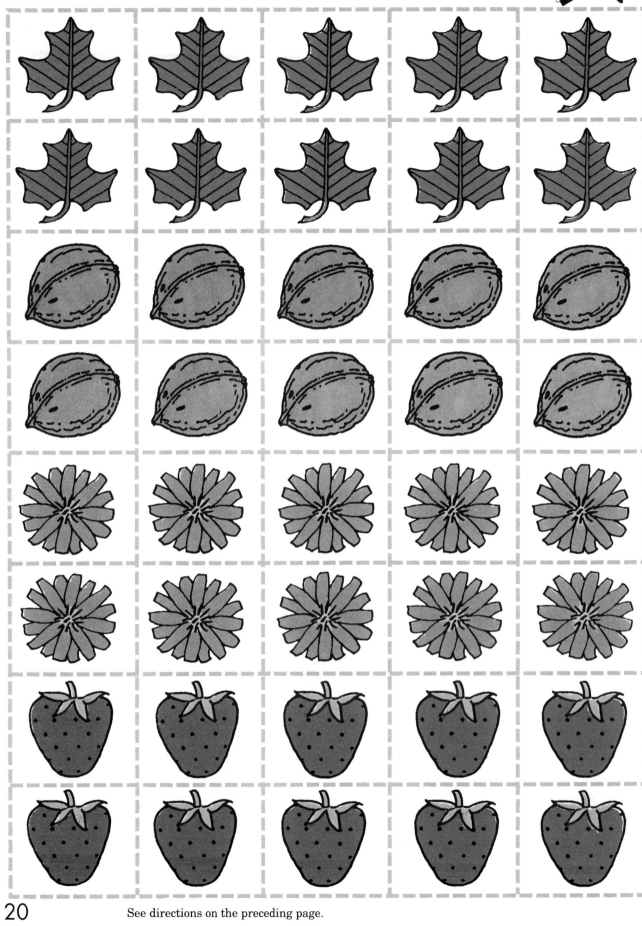

See directions on the preceding page.

Today we saw 7 yellow leaves.
Some of them blew away.
Print the possible number sentences.

$$7 - 2 = 5$$

There were 8 acorns in the basket.
The squirrels took some.
Print the possible number sentences.

$$8 - 1 = 7$$

Draw a story for 8 – 5 = 3.

Have the child use the pictures cut from pages 19 and 20 to make and record the possible number sentences.

21

We made a bouquet
of 9 flowers.
Some were pink.
Some were blue.
Print the possible number
sentences.

_____

_____

_____

_____

_____

_____

_____

_____

We made necklaces
of 10 berries.
Some were red.
Some were green.
Print the possible number
sentences.

_____

_____

_____

_____

_____

_____

_____

_____

Draw a story for 3 + 6 = 9.

Have the child use the pictures cut from pages 19 and 20 to make and
record the combinations of 9 and 10.

There were 9 flowers
in the garden. 🌸
Dill picked some.
Print the possible number
sentences.

_____

_____

_____

_____

_____

_____

_____

_____

Juniper collected
10 berries. 🍓
Then he ate some.
Print the possible number
sentences.

_____

_____

_____

_____

_____

_____

_____

_____

Draw a story for 10 − 4 = 6.

Have the child use the pictures cut from pages 19 and 20 to make and
record the possible number sentences.

23

_____

_____

_____

_____

_____

Have the child describe each story and record the corresponding number sentence.

_____

_____

How will you end this story?

Use as described on the preceding page. Discuss how the story might end and have the child draw the final scene and label it with a number sentence.

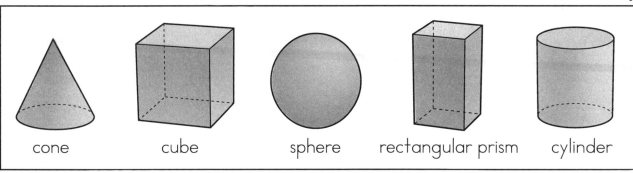

| cone | cube | sphere | rectangular prism | cylinder |

Date _____

I decided to look for _____

I found: _____

_____

_____

_____

_____

Then I looked for _____

I found: _____

_____

_____

_____

_____

What did you find the least of? Why?

_____

_____

_____

Have the child identify a solid and look for objects that have the same
shape. A recording of drawings, words or cut out pictures from magazines
can be used.

What do you think?
Will there be 2 windows
opposite the door?

_____

Will there be
a window opposite
the flower pot?

_____

Make the house
and find out.

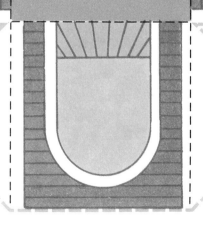

Have the child predict how the house will look before the net is cut and
glued together. To extend the activity, the child may wish to trace the net
and design her or his own house.

Whose House Is This?

28   This net can be used as an alternative to page 27. The child may wish
to draw features to make it a mouse house or a house for Trouble before
cutting and gluing it into a cube.

Use long straws, short straws, and Plasticine to build these models.

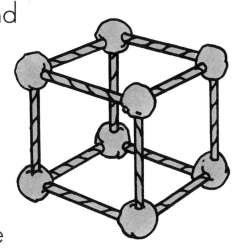

To build this I used:

_____ short straws

_____ balls of Plasticine

To build this I used:

_____  long straws

_____ short straws

_____ balls of Plasticine

Build your own model.   Draw your own model.

I used:

_____  long straws

_____  short straws

_____ balls of Plasticine

Discuss the instructions and illustrations with the child. Providing models of the geometric solids along with the straws and Plasticine would be beneficial for the child to observe and represent characteristics.

29

Collectors at Work

Tens

Ones

30   Have the child cut out the objects from pages 31 and 32 and arrange them on the mat to form sets to 99. The sets can be recorded on page 33. See page 93 for further direction.

The Store Room Supplies

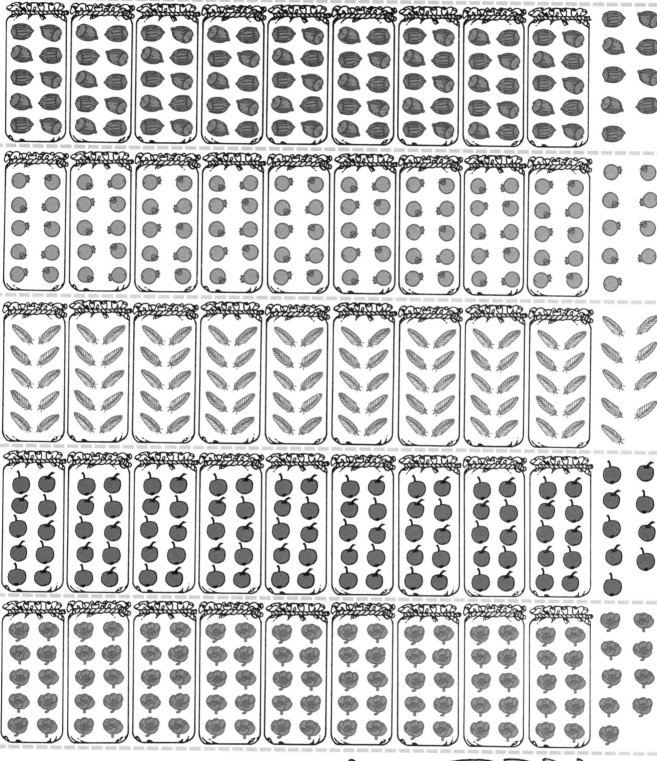

Use as described on page 30. You will need to store these in an envelope for further use on pages 34 and 35.

31

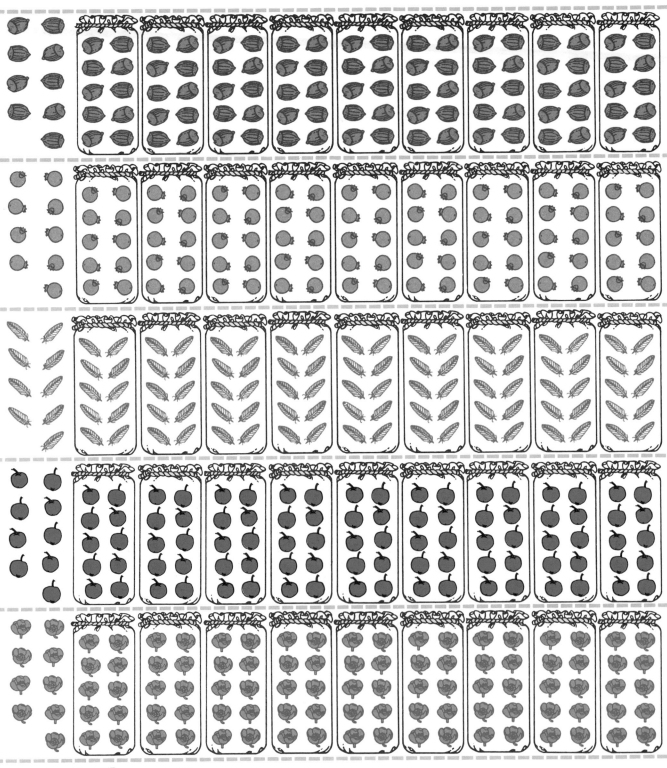

See directions on the preceding page.

Collector's Diary

Date	Tens	Ones	How many?
Sunday			
Monday			
Tuesday			
Wednesday			
Thursday			
Friday			
Saturday			

The sets created on page 30 can be recorded on this page. To extend the activity you might ask, **On which day did you collect the most objects? The least? Did you collect more on Monday or Wednesday?**

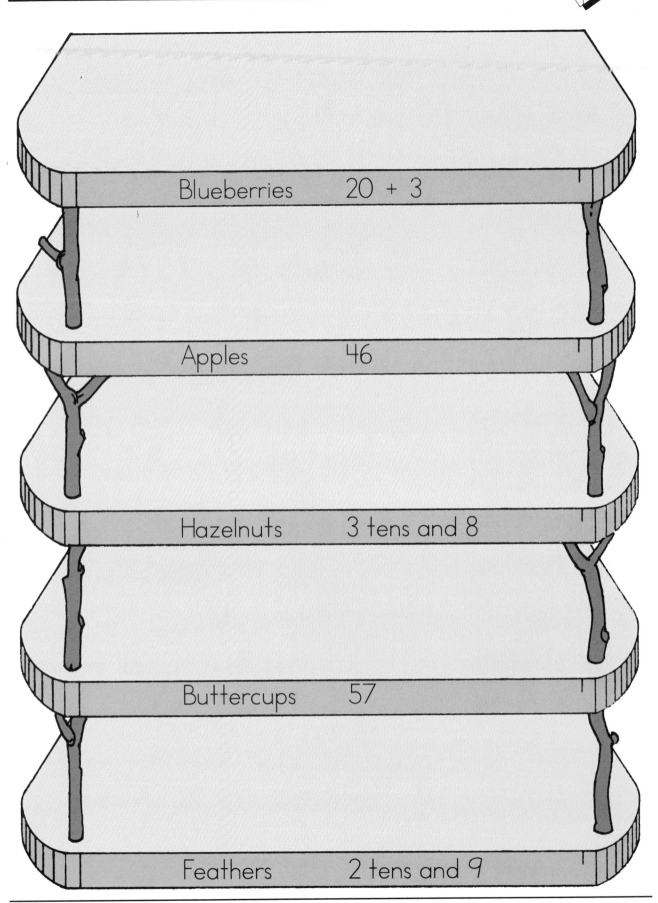

Blueberries   20 + 3

Apples   46

Hazelnuts   3 tens and 8

Buttercups   57

Feathers   2 tens and 9

Have the child glue objects cut from pages 31 and 32 so they represent the
numbers printed on these shelves.

Here are 10 hazelnuts.

How many hazelnuts do you think are here? _____
Circle groups of 10 to find out.

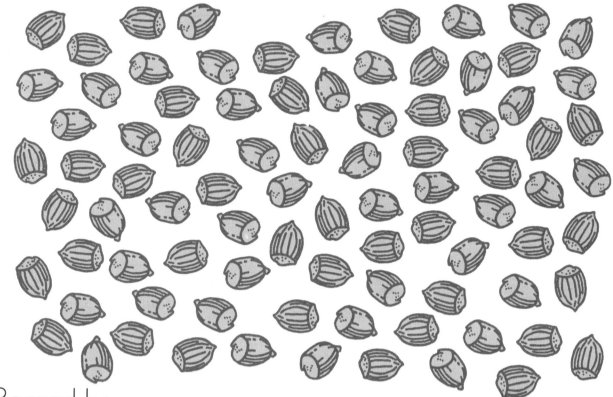

Record how many.

Store Room Log

_____ tens and _____ ones

_____ + _____

_____ hazelnuts

Have the child cover the collection of hazelnuts with a sheet of paper. Remove the paper and ask the child to look at the picture for 2 seconds. Cover the picture and then remove again for 2 seconds. Have the child record an estimate and then count the hazelnuts by circling groups of 10.

Have the child complete the clock to record what time it could be for each
picture and describe or write an accompanying sentence.

What do you do in the morning?

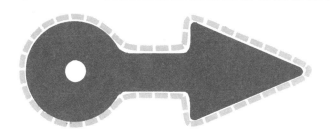 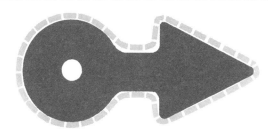

Have the child draw an event that he or she does at some time during the
morning. The clock is completed to show the approximate time of the event.
An accompanying story can be written or told. The hands can be cut and
secured to the clock on page 54.

My Information	_____ Information
What time do you wake up?	What time does your friend wake up?
_____	_____

Who wakes up earlier? _____

What time do you eat dinner?	What time does your friend eat dinner?
_____	_____

Who eats later? _____

If you ate an hour later, what time would it be? _____

What time do you go to bed?	What time does your friend go to bed?
_____	_____

What time do you like best? _____
Why do you like that time? _____

Have the child complete the appropriate questions and present the others to a friend. Have the child compare responses and record her or his observations.

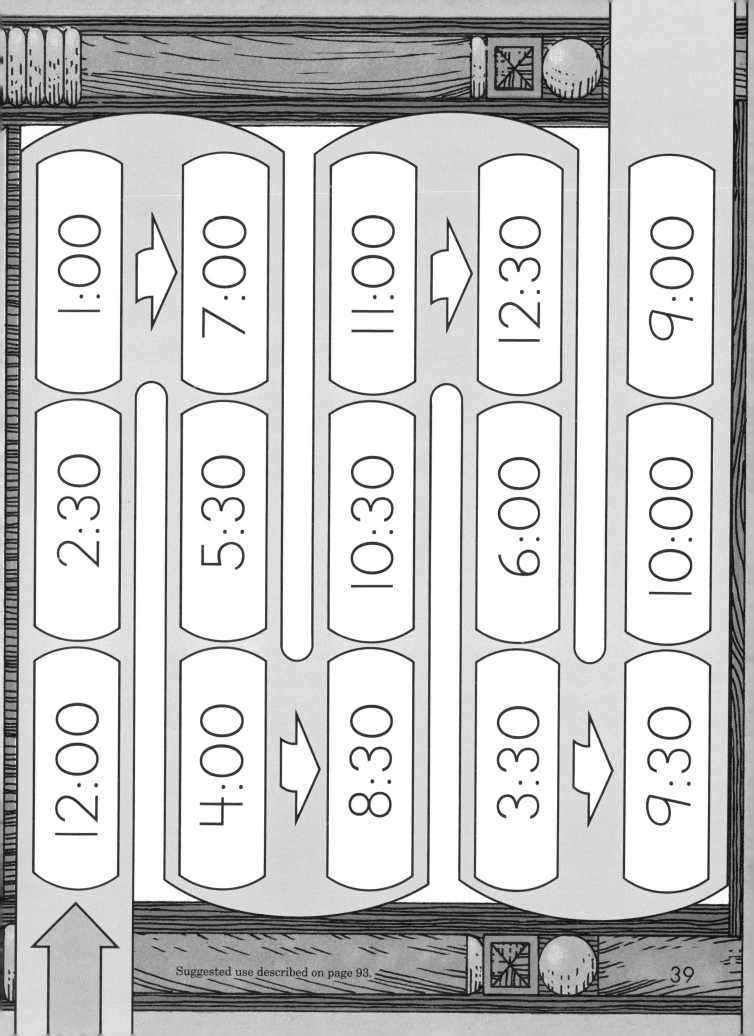

Suggested use described on page 93.

Suggested use described on page 94.

41

6	7	8	9	10
16	17	18	19	20
26	27	28	29	30
36	37	38	39	40
46	47	48	49	50
56	57	58	59	60
66	67	68	69	70
76	77	78	79	80
86	87	88	89	90
96	97	98	99	100

Suggested use described on page 94.

Graphing Mat

Suggested use described on page 94.

Game board

Suggested use described on page 93.

Suggested use described on page 93.

Sorting Mat

48   Suggested use described on page 94.

Suggested use described on page 94.

Hundreds Chart

1	2	3	4	5
11	12	13	14	15
21	22	23	24	25
31	32	33	34	35
41	42	43	44	45
51	52	53	54	55
61	62	63	64	65
71	72	73	74	75
81	82	83	84	85
91	92	93	94	95

Suggested use described on page 94.

Suggested use described on page 94.

51

Suggested use described on page 94.

Suggested use described on page 93.

53

Suggested use described on page 93.

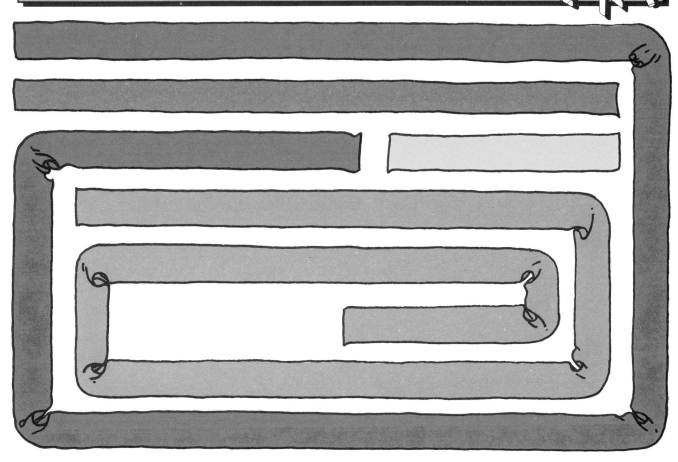

Which ribbon could you use to make a ring? _____

Which ribbon could you use to make a watch? _____

Which ribbon could you use to make a belt? _____

Which ribbon could you use to make

a headband? _____

Find something else that
is long enough to make a belt.

Find something else that is
as long as the watch ribbon.

Have the child estimate which ribbon is the appropriate length for each
item. The child may use a string to find out and answer the questions. Some
children may wish to make one of the items out of string and available
materials.

What could you buy for 14¢?

Shopping List

_____
_____
_____
_____
_____
_____
_____

What would you buy?

What could you buy for 12¢?

Shopping List

_____
_____
_____
_____
_____
_____
_____

What would you buy?

Have the child use the items cut from pages 57 and 58 to identify and record combinations of items that could be purchased for 14¢ and 12¢. A set of pictures can be glued onto the shopping bags to show what the child would buy for that amount.

Store Items

9¢

5¢

4¢

8¢

3¢

1¢

5¢

9¢

2¢

8¢

9¢

3¢

6¢

4¢

5¢

8¢

6¢

7¢

2¢

7¢

Have the child cut out the items for use with pages 56 and 59. Extra pieces
may be stored in an envelope or used to create a store display on a separate
piece of paper.

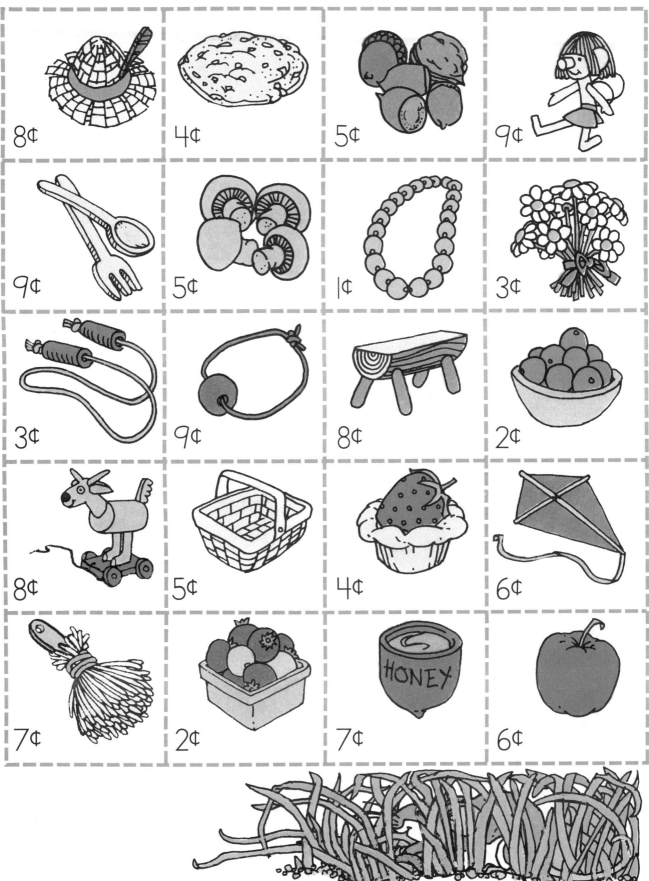

8¢

4¢

5¢

9¢

9¢

5¢

1¢

3¢

3¢

9¢

8¢

2¢

8¢

5¢

4¢

6¢

7¢

2¢

7¢

6¢

See directions on the preceding page.

What could you buy for _____ ¢?

Shopping List

_____
_____
_____
_____
_____
_____

What would you buy?

What could you buy for _____ ¢?

Shopping List

_____
_____
_____
_____
_____
_____

What would you buy?

Have the child record selected or given amounts on the piggy bank labels. Have the child use the items cut from pages 57 and 58 to identify and record combinations of items that could be purchased for the amounts. Pictures can be glued onto the shopping bags to show what the child would buy.

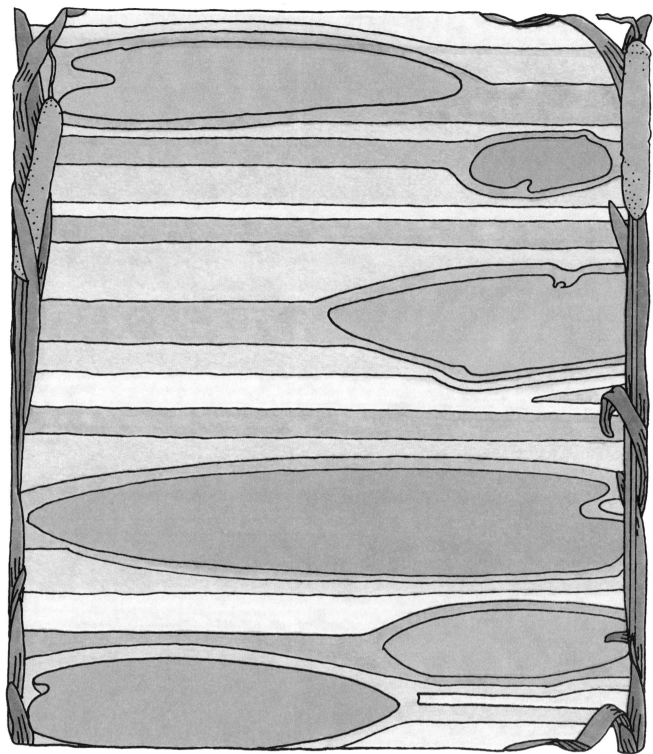

There were 16 frogs on lily pads.
6 jumped into the water.
How many are still on lily pads? _____

Have the child use the frogs cut from page 61 to act out the stories. The child may record her or his response by printing a sentence or a number sentence.

There were 7 frogs at the pond.
8 more frogs hopped to the pond too.
How many frogs are at the pond?

There were 6 frogs.
9 frogs joined them.
How many frogs are at the pond?

There were 13 frogs on lily pads.
6 went swimming.
How many frogs are on lily pads now?

There were 5 frogs on lily pads.
9 more came.
How many frogs are
on lily pads altogether?

There were 16 frogs at the pond.
7 left.
How many frogs are still at the pond?

Use as described on the preceding page. The child may wish to glue frog
pictures on the pond work mat to represent one of the stories.

61

Animal Adventures

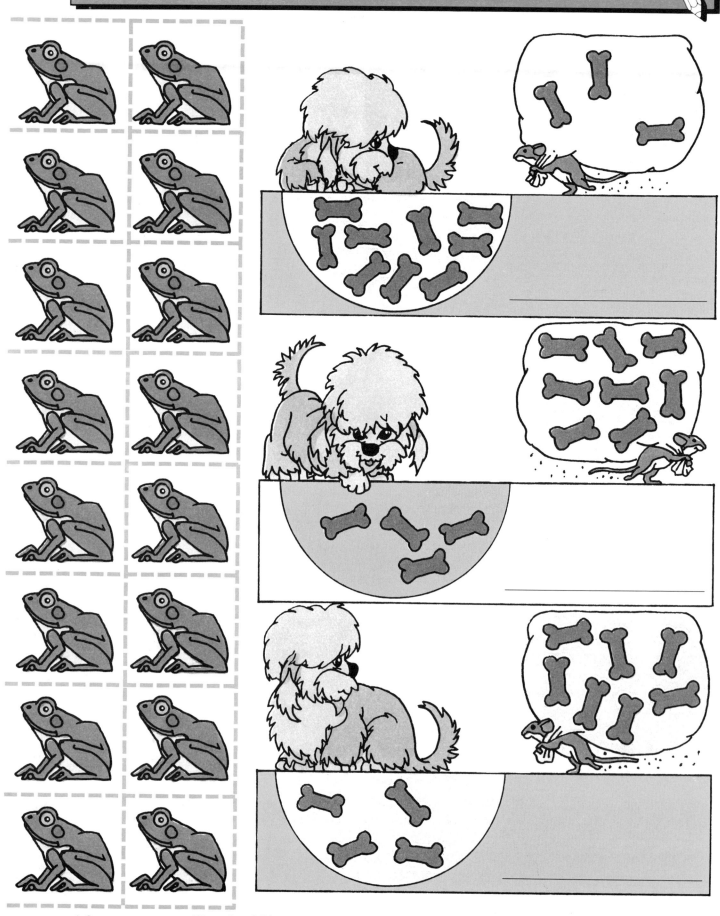

Have the child record a caption for each event in the filmstrip story. The child can write a caption or print a corresponding number sentence. Encourage the child to describe the story.

Then ...

Use as described on the preceding page. Discuss how the last story might end and have the child draw the final scene and write the caption or label it with a number sentence.

63

Figure Graph

Triangle   Circle   Square   Rectangle

Which figure did
you see the most? _____

Which figure did
you see the least? _____

What else did you
learn from your graph? _____

Have the child look around to find circles, squares, triangles, and rectangles in the environment. A picture may be drawn in the appropriate column to record her or his observations. Discuss the results of the graph with the child.

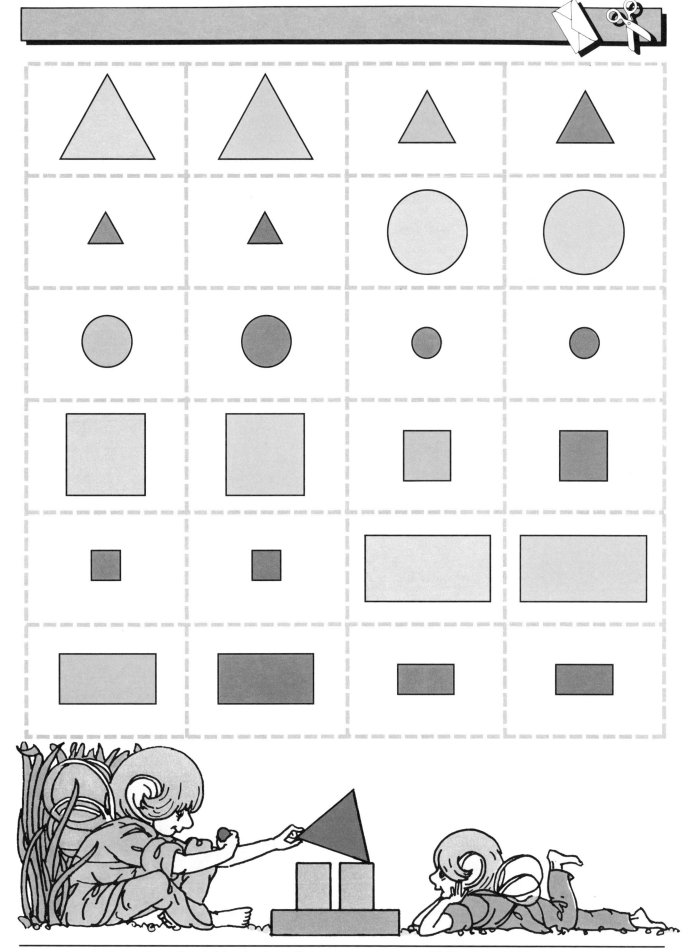

Have the child cut out the figures for use on page 67. You may wish to store these figures in an envelope and use them for sorting or patterning activities prior to working with page 67.

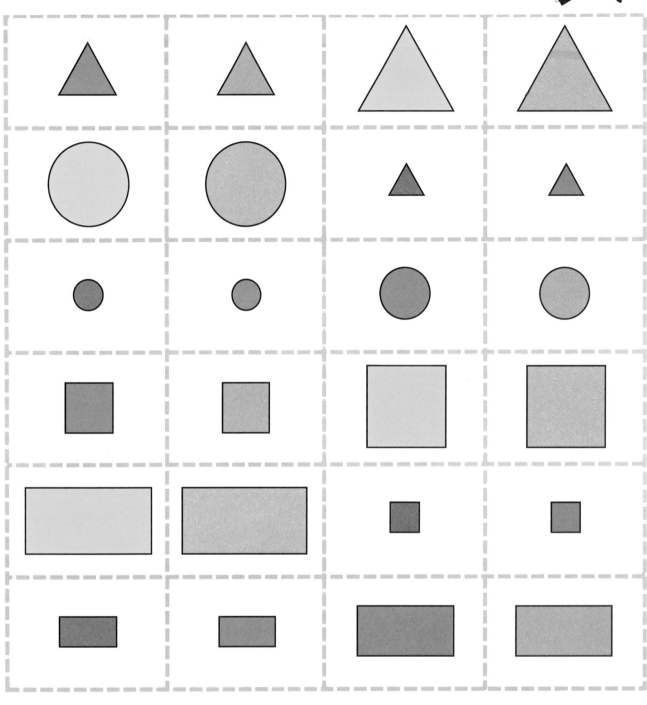

See directions on the preceding page.

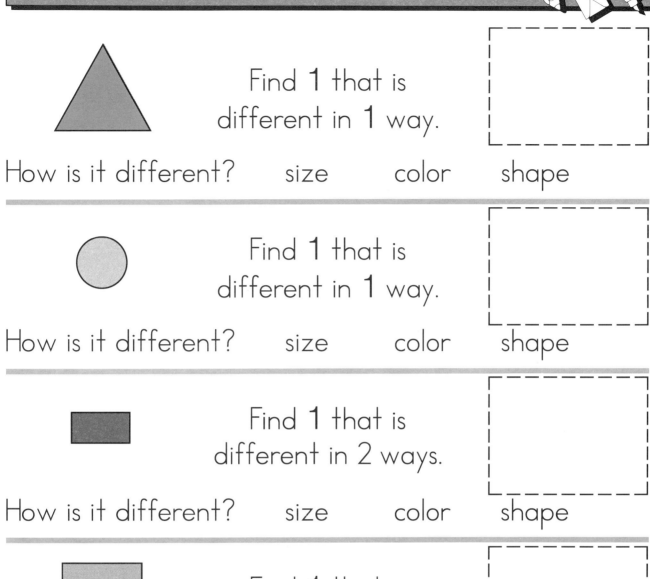

Find **1** that is different in **1** way.

How is it different?   size   color   shape

Find **1** that is different in **1** way.

How is it different?   size   color   shape

Find **1** that is different in **2** ways.

How is it different?   size   color   shape

Find **1** that is different in **2** ways.

How is it different?   size   color   shape

Have the child find figures cut from pages 65 and 66 in response to these
problems. Have the child glue the figure into the blank square and circle
the attribute(s) to identify how the figure is different. Encourage the child
to explain her or his choices.

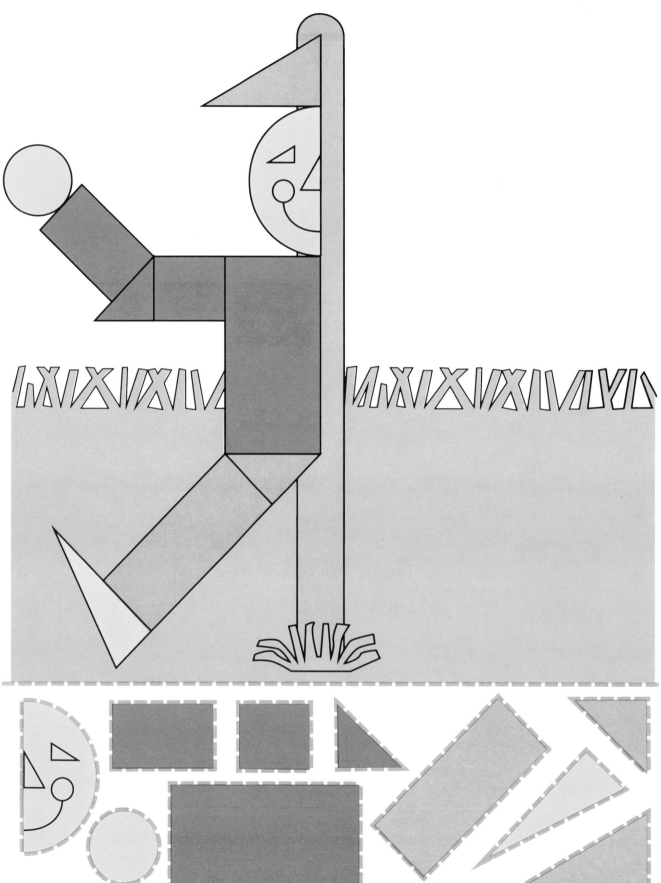

68

Have the child cut out the pieces and arrange them beside the scarecrow to create a symmetrical image. A mirror can be used to check the image before gluing the pieces in place.

Pizza Toppings

mushrooms   pepperoni   onion   tomato   bacon   pineapple

Special Order

$\frac{1}{2}$ bacon

$\frac{1}{2}$ pineapple

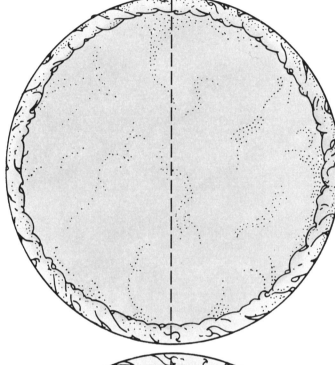

Special Order

$\frac{1}{4}$ pepperoni

$\frac{1}{4}$ onion

$\frac{2}{4}$ mushrooms

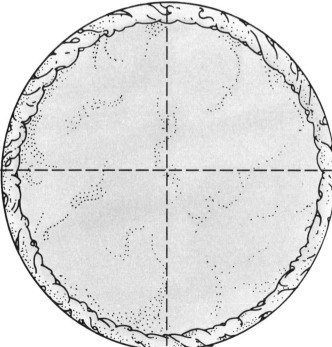

Have the child create special order pizzas by drawing toppings of the specified portions.

69

Today's Special!: Ten Slice Pizza
Place your order here!

Special Order

_____   _____

_____   _____

_____   _____

_____   _____

Have the child complete the order form by recording the toppings and the
fraction. Have the child draw the toppings on the appropriate portions and
the fraction. The child may refer to the menu on page 69 or create her or
his own toppings.

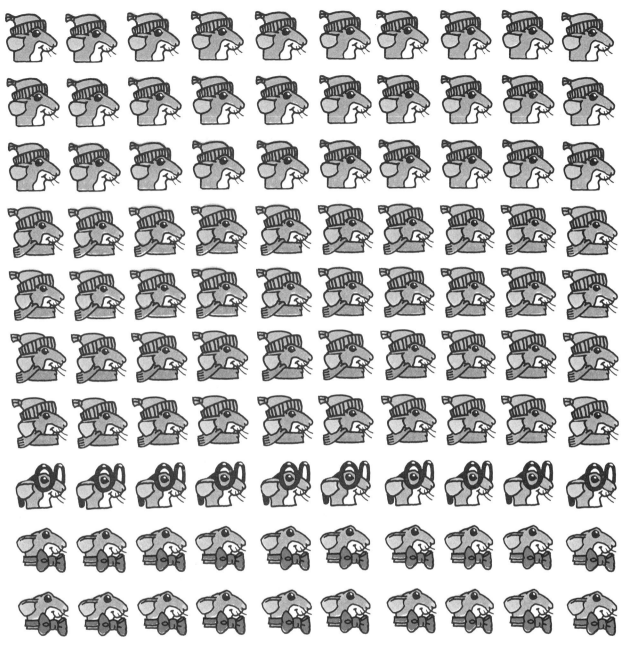

How many mice do you think there are?　＿＿＿＿＿＿

How many mice are wearing glasses?　＿＿＿＿＿＿

How many mice are wearing scarves?　＿＿＿＿＿＿

How many mice are wearing green hats?　＿＿＿＿＿＿

How many mice are wearing bow ties?　＿＿＿＿＿＿

Have the child estimate and record how many mice he or she thinks are on
the page before examining the page closely. Have the child respond to the
questions. Encourage the child to describe or record other observations.

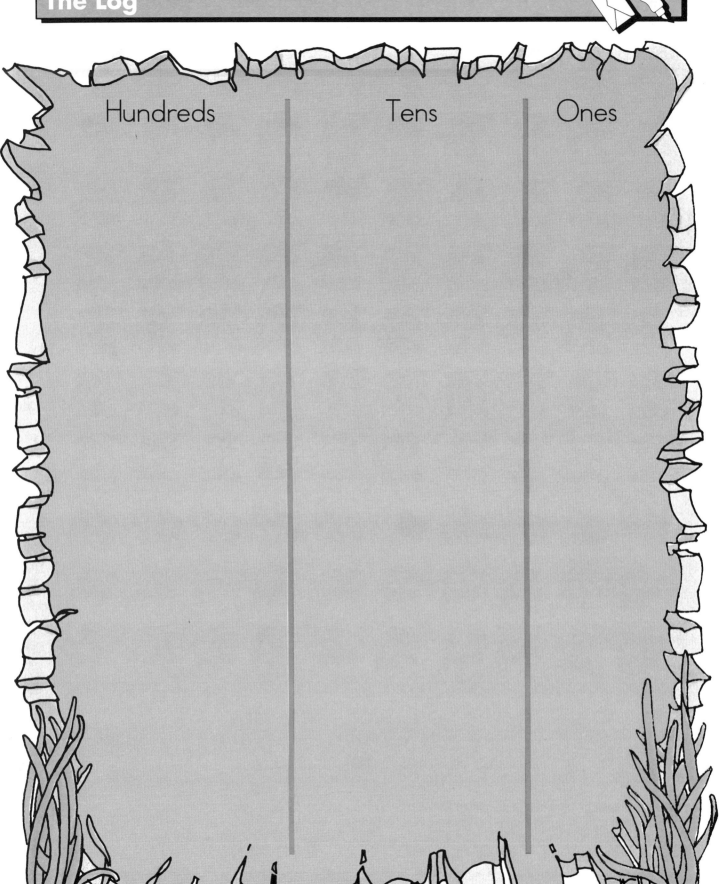

Hundreds   Tens   Ones

Have the child cut out the objects from pages 73 and 74 and arrange them in the log to form sets to 999. The sets can be recorded on page 75.

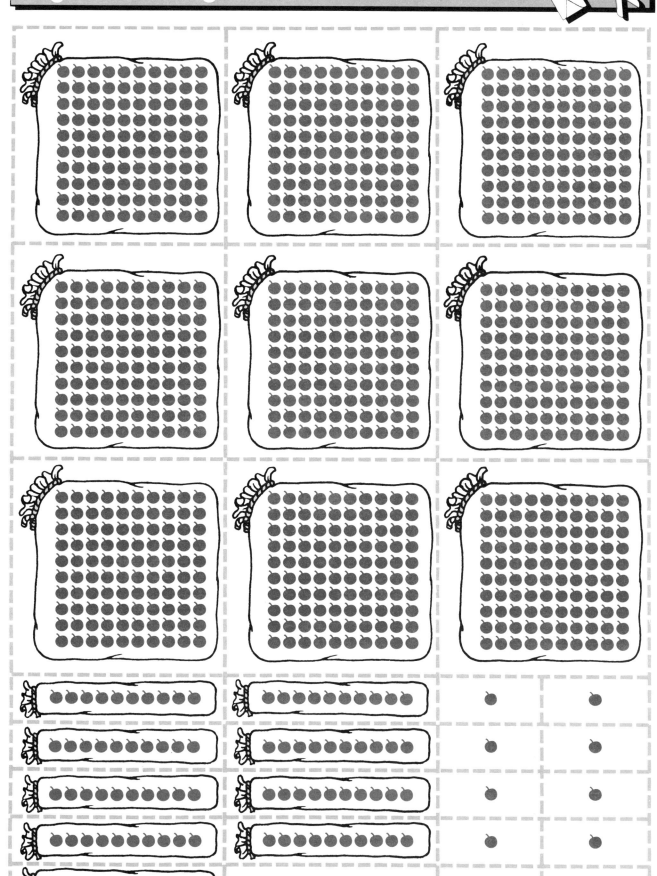

Use as directed on page 72. You may wish to store these in an envelope for
further use on pages 76 and 77.

Bags for the Log Room

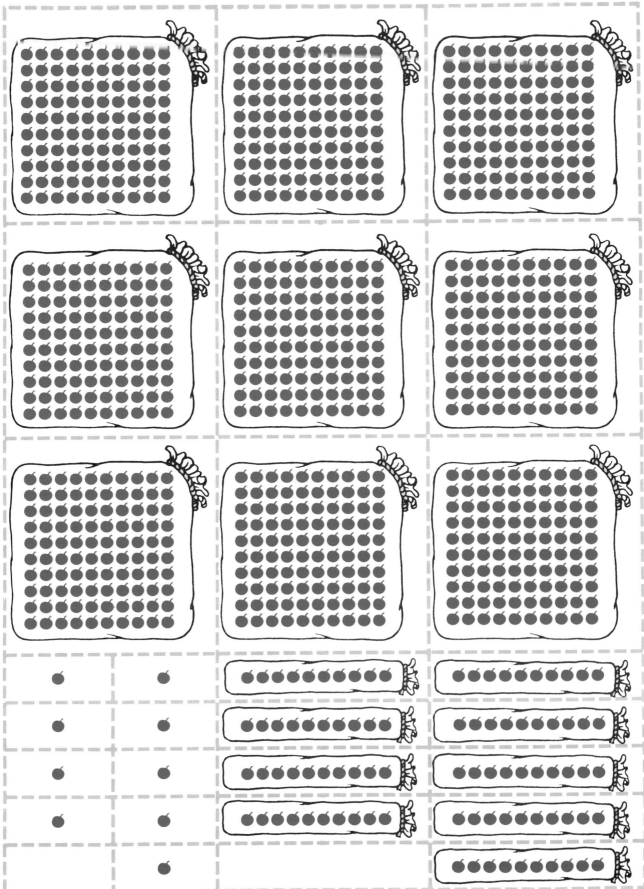

74   See directions on the preceding page.

Month	Hundreds	Tens	Ones	How Many?
January				
February				
March				
April				
May				
June				
July				
August				
September				
October				
November				
December				

The sets created on page 72 can be recorded on this page. To extend the activity you might ask, **In which month did you collect the most? The least? In which months did you collect more than October? Less?**

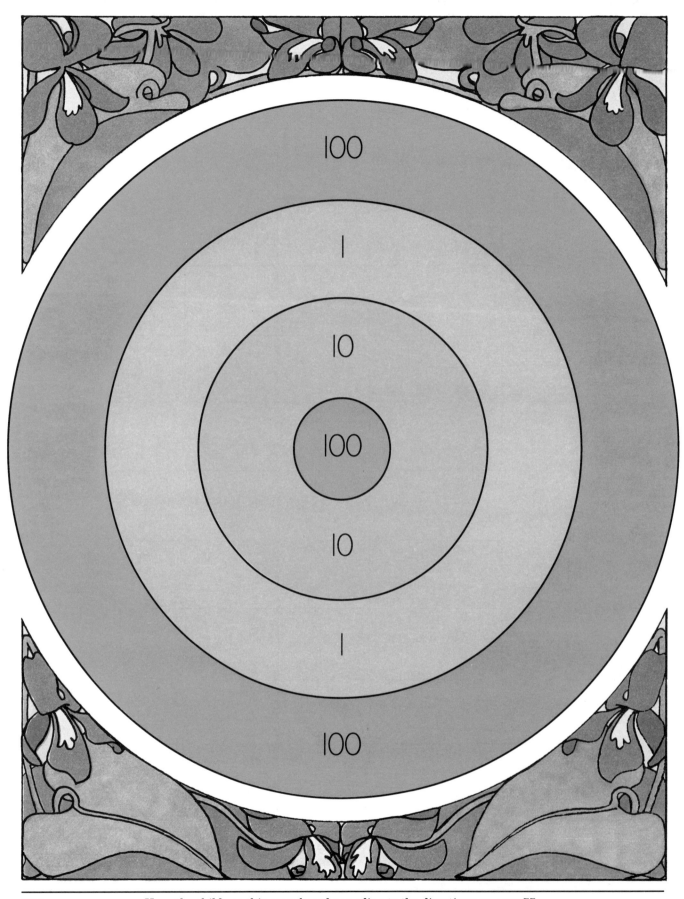

Have the child use this score board according to the directions on page 77.
The cut outs from pages 73 and 74 may be used when adding up the total
score for each game.

First game: Drop 5 markers.   Score _____

Second game: Drop 5 markers.   Score _____

Third game: Drop 6 markers.   Score _____

Fourth game: Drop 7 markers   Score _____

Fifth game: Drop 7 markers.   Score _____

Was your first game more or
less than your second game?   _____

Which game had the highest score?   _____

Which game had the lowest score?   _____

Have the child hold the markers a reasonable distance above the target on
page 76. The child opens her or his hand to drop the markers. Have the
child compare the scores for each game and record her or his observations.

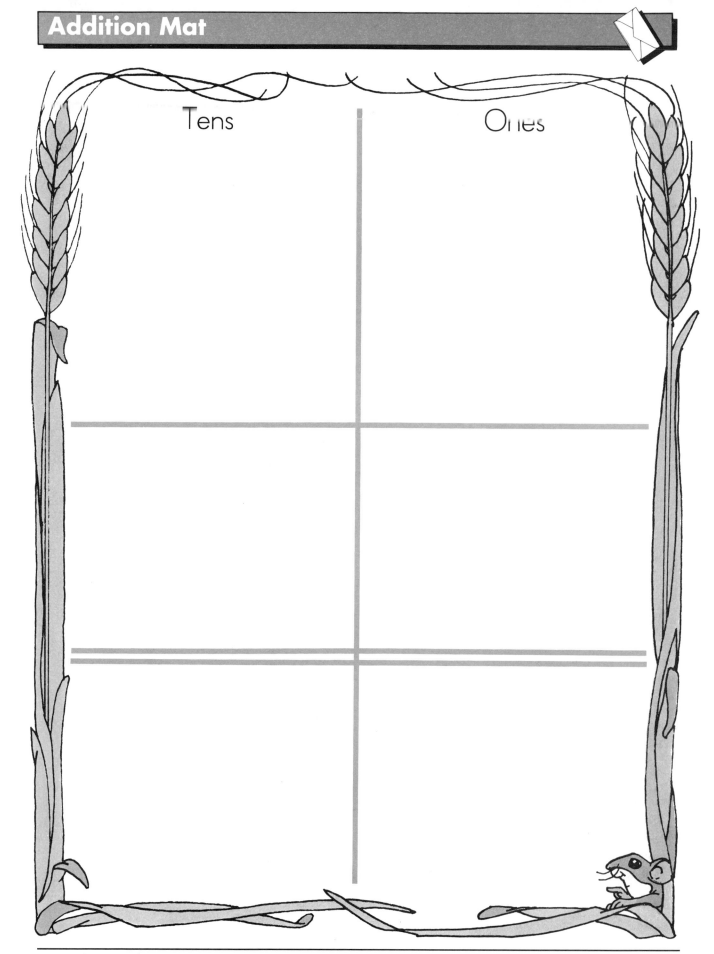

Tens | Ones

Have the child use the cut outs from pages 79 and 80 to answer the story
problems presented on page 81. The two sets are arranged on the mat and
joined together in the bottom section of the mat.

Beansticks and Cubes

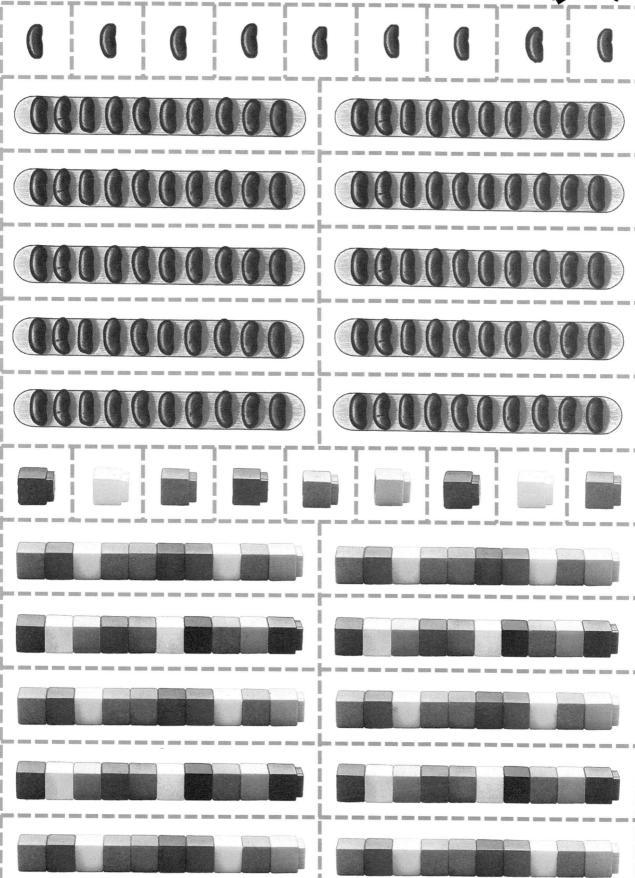

Have the child cut out the materials and arrange sets on the addition mat
on page 78 to act out the problems presented on pages 81, 83, and 84.

79

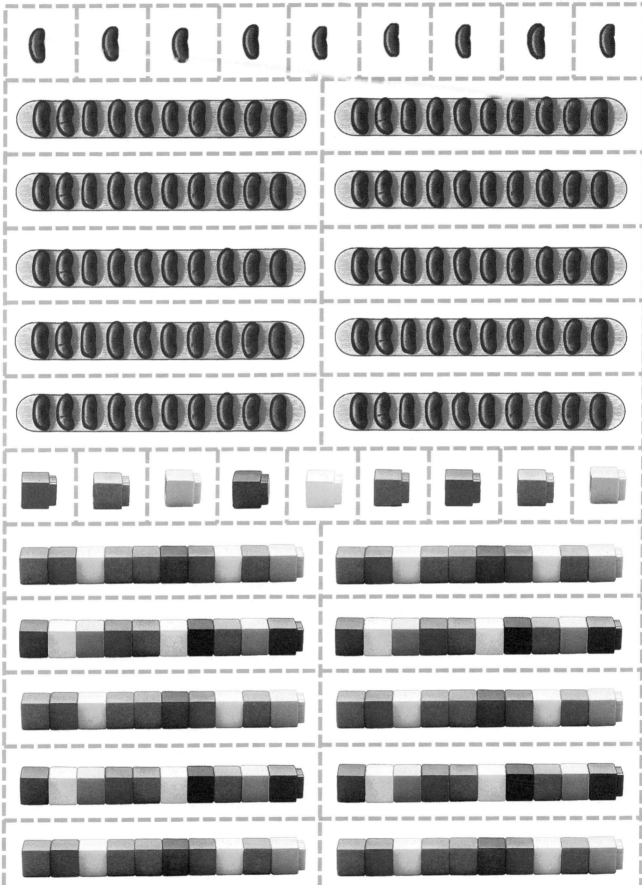

Use as described on the preceding page.

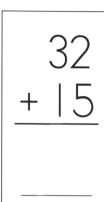

$$\begin{array}{r} 32 \\ + 15 \\ \hline \end{array}$$

My story: _____

_____

_____

_____

_____

$$\begin{array}{r} \underline{} \\ + \underline{} \\ \hline \end{array}$$

My story: _____

_____

_____

_____

_____

Have the child create a story problem for each additive situation. The cut outs from pages 79 and 80 can be used on the addition mat, page 78, to solve the problems.

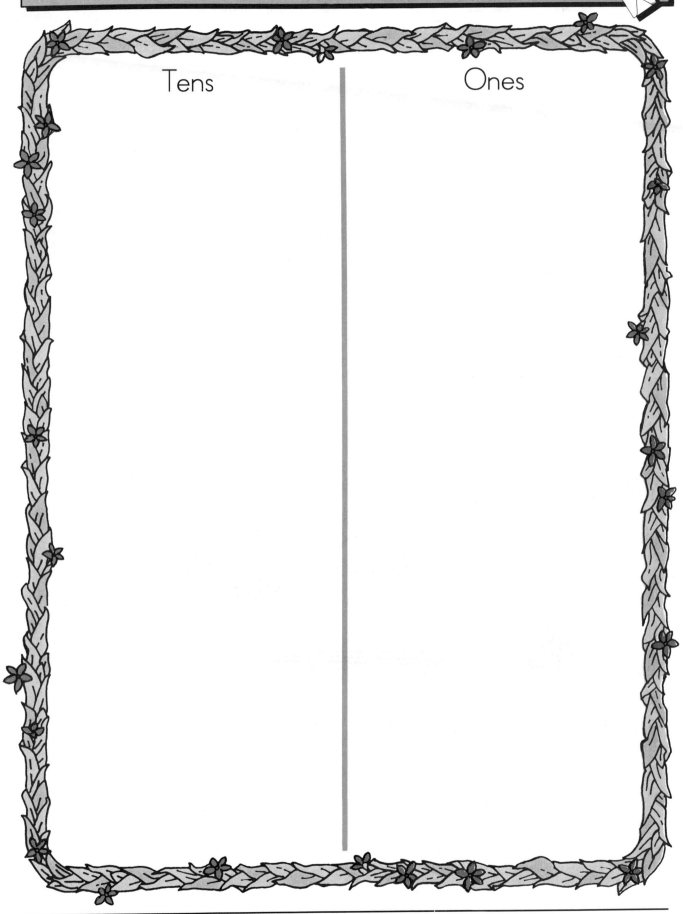

Tens

Ones

Have the child use the cut outs from pages 79 and 80 to answer the problems presented on page 83. The set is arranged on the place value mat and the appropriate set is removed.

Story Problems

85¢

36¢   74¢   28¢   69¢

My story: _____

_____

_____

_____

_____

MUFFINS FOR SALE

Muffins 64   37 sold

My story: _____

_____

_____

_____

_____

Have the child create a story problem for each subtractive situation. The cut outs from pages 79 and 80 can be used on the place value mat, page 82, to solve the problems.

83

Cross-Number Puzzle

	1				2	3	
4			5	6		7	8
		9					
	10				11		
12					13	14	
		15		16		17	
		18		19	20		
21					22		

Across

1.	66 – 55	12.	77 – 30
2.	27 – 14	13.	75 – 48
4.	69 – 20	17.	16 + 14
5.	24 + 35	19.	34 + 41
7.	58 + 19	21.	27 + 13
10.	42 + 42	22.	91 – 22

Down

1.	98 – 79	10.	38 + 49
3.	78 – 41	11.	84 – 52
4.	25 + 21	12.	60 – 19
6.	41 + 52	14.	21 + 52
8.	85 – 13	15.	66 + 26
9.	27 + 27	16.	98 – 81
		20.	51 + 5

84   Have the child use the cut outs from pages 79 and 80 to complete the cross-number puzzle.

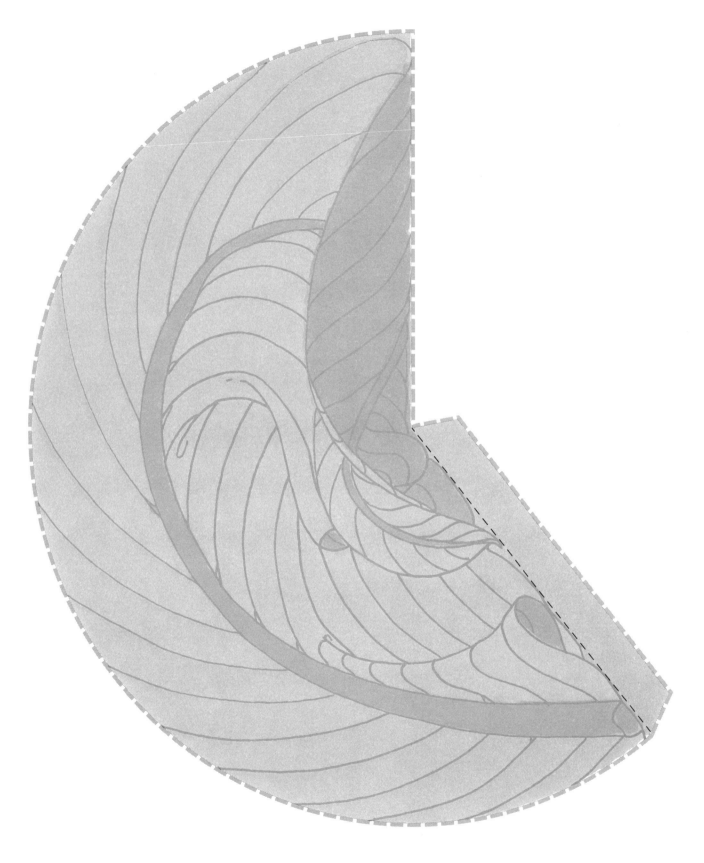

Have the child cut and paste the net to form a cone. Use with page 87.

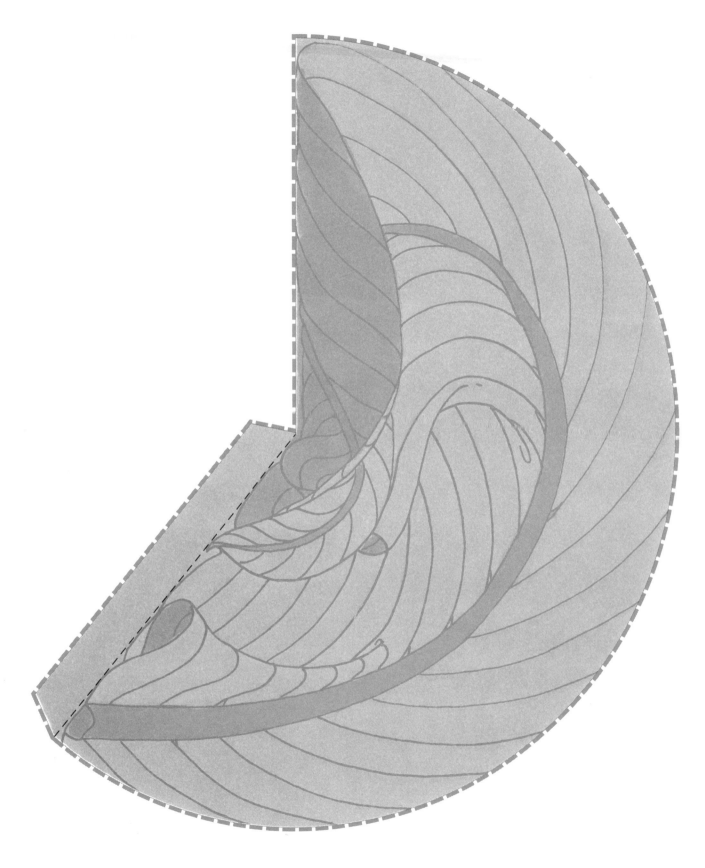

Follow the directions on the preceding page.

Fill your cone with rice, sand,
flour, beans or _____

Find things that hold more than your cone.

I found: _____

_____

_____

_____

_____

Find things that hold less.

I found: _____

_____

_____

_____

_____

Does your hand hold more or less? _____

Use the cone made from pages 85 and 86. Have the child complete the
activities described and record her or his observations. Encourage the child
to discuss her or his thinking before and after the investigation.

87

Make 3 plates of 2 cookies.

How many cookies? _____

Make 4 bags of 2 marbles.

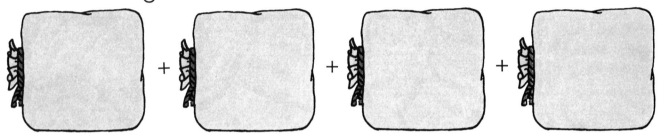

How many marbles? _____

Make 5 boxes of 2 toys.

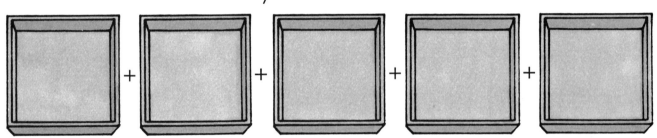

How many toys? _____

Make 5 trays of 3 muffins.

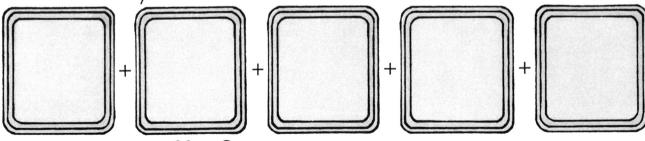

How many muffins? _____

Have the child arrange the cut out pictures from pages 89 and 90 as described for each question. Encourage the child to record discoveries and describe her or his thinking.

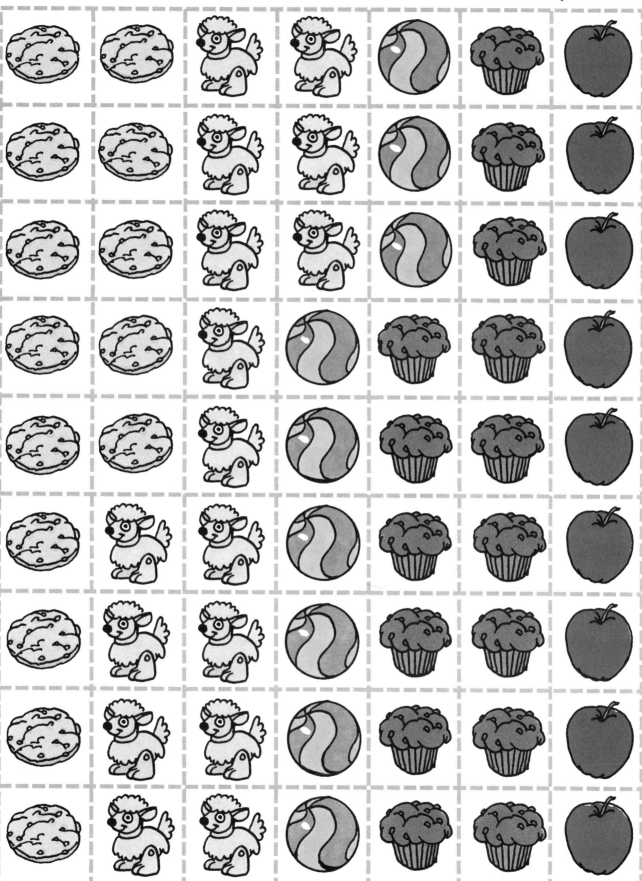

Have the child cut out the objects and arrange them as described on pages 88 and 92. You may wish to store the pictures in an envelope.

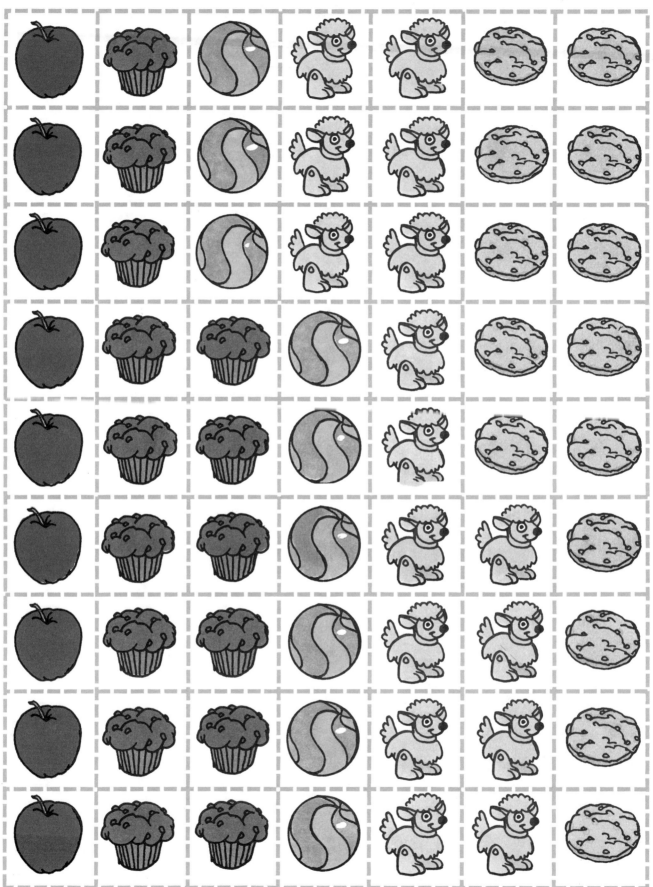

See directions on the preceding page.

Look at these Zogs!

5 zogs.
How many antennae? _____

2 zogs.
How many legs? _____

3 zogs.
How many eyes? _____

5 zogs.
How many mouths? _____

4 zogs.
How many antennae? _____

Make up your own question.

_____

_____

_____

_____

_____

_____

Have the child examine the zogs to answer each question. The child can
respond by drawing or writing. Some children may enjoy making up their
own creatures and answering the same question.

Share 8 cookies.

How many Burritts? _____

How many for each? _____

Share 4 cookies.

How many Burritts? _____

How many for each? _____

Share 12 muffins.

How many Burritts? _____

How many for each? _____

Share 8 apples between 2 Burritts.

How many for each?

_____

Share 9 apples among 3 Burritts.

How many for each?

_____

Have the child arrange the pictures cut from pages 89 and 90 to act out these situations. The child may respond in several ways, e.g., drawing or writing. The child may wish to create her or his own questions or glue down the pictures to represent one of the given situations.

Puppets (pages 3 to 10)
and Zogs (pages 11 and 12)

Puppets and/or zogs can be used to

- act out stories, songs, and poems from *Explorations 2* and those known or created by the children,
- act out and solve story problems related to a variety of number concepts. For example, create combinations for a number, 9 and 2, 8 and 3, 7 and 4, 6 and 3 etc., choose the correct operation, e.g., *6 zogs came to talk to Dill and then 6 more joined them. How many zogs are with Dill? What is the number sentence?* $(6 + 6 = 12)$ *3 groups of 2 zogs were in the field. How many zogs were there?* $(3 \times 2 = 6)$

All puppets can be used in plays while the zogs (pages 11 and 12) can also be used on the story boards (pages 41-52 and 42-51) to reinforce many mathematics ideas. For example a child could

- sort and re-sort the zogs,
- create and describe patterns made with the zogs,
- use the zog pictures to create and solve addition, subtraction, and multiplication sentences,
- use the zogs as markers or game pieces for the game boards (pages 40-53 and 46-47).

Clock (pages 39 and 54)

Have the child secure the hands cut from page 37 to the clock face (page 54) with a butterfly tack. The clock can be used to demonstrate different times identified through stories, daily events, or verbal instructions. The children can play a game using the digital clocks as a game board. Each player places her or his marker on the starting arrow. The first player rolls a numbered cube and moves the marker ahead. The child reads the time he or she landed on aloud. Instructions can then vary depending upon the skill you wish to reinforce. For example, the child could create the appropriate time on the clock face or describe an event that could happen at that time. To challenge some children, you may wish to ask them to identify one hour later or one hour earlier on the clock face.

Game Boards (pages 40-53 and 46-47)
Game Pieces (pages 19 and 20, 31 and 32, 73 and 74, and 79 and 80)

To form a large game board, have two children join their boards together, one using pages 40 and 53 and the other using pages 46 and 47.

The pictures cut from pages 19 and 20 can be used in games to create sets and demonstrate addition, subtraction, or multiplication sentences. The place value pictures cut from pages 31 and 32, 73 and 74, and 79 and 80 can be used in games that reinforce 2-digit and 3-digit number concepts. Many games can be created to reinforce addition and subtraction.

- Have the child make 2 sets of numeral cards for 0 to 9. The cards should be mixed and placed face down. A child spins the spinner. Before the marker is moved ahead, the child turns over 2 numeral cards and completes a predetermined task. For example, the child could use the 2 numbers to create an addition or subtraction sentence, identify and solve 2 related addition sentences; tell a subtraction or addition story; etc. If the other players agree that the task has been completed, the child moves the marker to the next colored space that corresponds to the spinner.
- The procedure above could be adapted for work with place value. For example, establish that one of the cards is a tens card and the other card turned over is a ones card. The child could form a 2-digit number with the 2 cards and complete a task such as the following before moving a marker forward:
  - identify the number and create the set,
  - identify the number before and after,
  - count on or back 10 numbers,
  - form the greater (less) number with the 2 cards, etc.
- For reinforcing 3-digit numbers have the players select 3 numeral cards and encourage the children to create their own games.

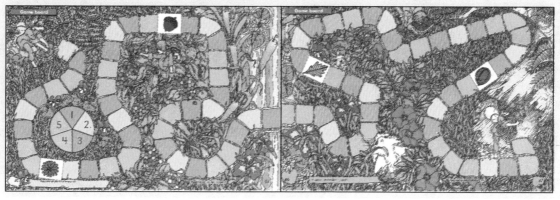

Story Boards (pages 41-52 and 42-51)

Story boards may be used to reinforce a wide range of number skills. Have the children use the puppets (pages 9 and 10), the zogs (pages 11 and 12), the pictures cut from pages 19 and 20, or counters to act out story situations which involve any of the number concepts described.

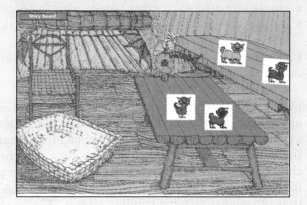

Hundreds Chart (pages 43 and 50)

The hundreds chart can be used to
- count by ones, twos, fives, and tens. Encourage the child to talk about the pattern,
- count by tens beginning at any numeral on the top row, e.g., 7, 17, 27... Talk about the pattern,
- cover even numbers to identify odd numbers and vice versa. Talk about the pattern,
- find and describe other counting patterns.

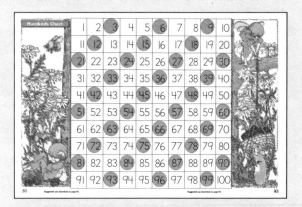

- count on or back 10 from a given number,
- identify the missing numerals when a row or a random selection have been covered,
- find mystery numbers, e.g., the number is greater than 80, less than 95 and you say it when counting by tens. What is it?
- play a game with the left over tens and ones from pages 79 and 80. The player rolls a numbered cube and moves her or his marker ahead the number indicated. He or she then creates the number landed on with the cut outs.

Graphing Mat (pages 44 and 49)

- Pose a question or have the child create a question related to a topic of interest. Begin by creating and talking about concrete graphs. Later have the child create pictographs and bar graphs.
- Asking questions similar to these will assist the child in interpreting the graphs.
  - *Which column has more? less? or do they have the same number?*
  - *Are there more (less) ___ than ___ ?*
  - *How many more (less) ___ are there than ___ ?*
  - *What else can you tell me about your graph?*

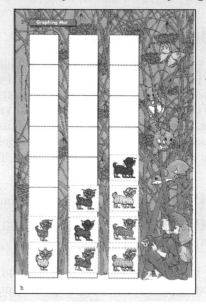

Sorting Mat (pages 45 and 48)

Provide the child with a variety of materials to sort. Have the child
- sort a set of objects, e.g., all the paper things,
- sort everything in the group by one attribute (or two attributes) e.g., color, shape, size, texture.
- sort and re-sort the objects.

These questions may be asked:
- *How did you sort these?*
- *Why does (doesn't) this belong here?*
- *What other way could you sort these? Show me.*

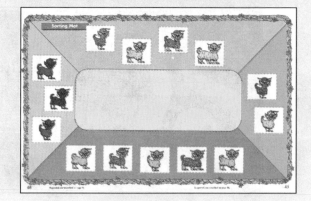